DUSK

TILL

MOAN

FROM DUSK TILL MOAN

FreedomInk Publishing

P.O Box 1093 Reidsville Georgia 30453

This book is a compilation of erotic poetry respectively submitted by each Author/Poet herein listed. Each Author/Poet has given their express permission to publish their works within this book.

Cover Designer: Elaina Lee at For the Muse

ISBN: 978-0-9896786-9-8

FROM DUSK TILL MOAN

TABLE OF CONTENTS

HOLMZIE DA GOD...
Introduction

PHOENIX...
Yoni Affirmation

Satisfaction

July

Extreme Content

Grand Rising

Seduction

ANU...
Every Morning

Fuck you/fuck you

Thirsty

#Mood

PSA (Paranormal Sexual Activity)

Lunchbreak

Star Gazers

FROM DUSK TILL MOAN

DANOVEL...
View You
Little Vicky Secret
Sexual Alignment
Lust At Dawn

JA'MAELA BYRD WRITING AS ARIA KNOX...
Collide
Danger Zone
Fleshy Fruit
G Spot
Untitled

K.SHANEL...
Good Till The Last...
Pussy Pics
Love Slave
Climax

VINO DAVIS...
3:33

FROM DUSK TILL MOAN

FROM DUSK TILL MOAN

INTRO

Chasing the euphoria you had once before. That first time so perfect. You've been on the hunt for more. It awakens you before the sunlight. At night your satisfaction escapes you as your presence competes with the moon. Your body leaps to a mood.... Weak and unsteady you swoon Overwhelmed. Insomniac. No sleep in this room.

You can't quite recall... Was it a touch, a caress, a kiss? But trust, once it's in your grasp once more you'll know what it is. As you dive into memory, you realize this world is your newfound home. Erogenous zones of the body AND soul. Can't get enough as your mind is repeatedly blown.

From sun up to sun down you'll long for it. And just what is it? That is unknown. Still you'll lust, you'll groan... From dusk till moan.

~HOLMZIE DA GOD

FROM DUSK TILL MOAN

FROM DUSK TILL MOAN

I reign seduction, and it's exactly what it seems... ~Phoenix

FROM DUSK TILL MOAN

FROM DUSK TILL MOAN

YONI AFFIRMATION

Unpurified thoughts that reach the impossible
Confessions of Erotic Vixen, the Audible
Daily quotes and body translation
I don't have to be naked for masturbation
I need ME to manifest my intentions
Sweat beading releasing my tensions
Benefiting and cultivating the highest good
Making love to myself more than anyone could
Relinquishing fears and purging my frustration
Orgasms that knock me off my foundation
I am fucking brilliant and overcum with joy
Skills I am certainly qualified to deploy
I forgive those who have harmed me in my past
And peacefully wash away
and detach with all of my ability
I exude feminine generative power
This majestic delicacy doesn't sour
Where only the divine can devour
I promise my lushness won't cower
With every entry, no X marked exit
Only a cosmic free fall into the infinite
I affirm

~PHOENIX

SATISFACTION

Your physique stunned me into silence
And your intoxication would have me losing my license
I demand penetration under and over me
Intense breathing melodic and off-key
Moaning insanely
with glistening bodies feasting on every crevice
With juices trickling down these thick ass thighs.
I fucking love us.
I watch as you feast on my drenched peach
Anticipating your next move
Deliberate clit massages like you got something to prove
Grinding my hips against you
Headhunter, no need for the vibrator
I am the buffet, and you are the Caterer
Soaked with cum and spit, I tip my head back
Pretending to be and erotic scene from Chyna Black
Eat. Fuck. Sleep.
Tapping me with your throbbing muscle,
It's time to do it again
I guess you're turning me out,
because I'm not even into men
Taking you into my mouth so you can stroke my throat
Giving your mic the greatest speech, I ever wrote
I don't want to miss one drop of your sticky sweets
Sucking on the head I salaciously greet
Slobbering good trouble awaiting your release

FROM DUSK TILL MOAN

Working my miles, fucked if this is leased
Eat. Fuck. Sleep.
You've restricted me to that regimen
Don't get too cocky because I'm feminine
Thrusting in and out faster, waiting for the money shot
Cumming deeper than the camera caught
I hope you're satisfied...

~PHOENIX

FROM DUSK TILL MOAN

JULY

It was the hottest that it's ever been
Not a breeze in sight, no air conditioning
You leaned in to give me the kiss I've been waiting for
Solidifying the feelings that I denied I'm sure
You would think I was your whore
Had me spread out all over the floor
Your tongue entered my sacred spaces
Fingering my adult places
Then you conquered my body with your joystick
Our encounter was certainly nothing quick
I didn't give up, I wasn't going to lose this bout
Every time you slide it in and drag it out
My moans intensify never wanting this to end
Slobbering on you as my eyes grow with anticipation
My erotic nature wants you to finish on my face
I want it nasty baby, a complete disgrace
But there was a passion we didn't intend on
Going 4 rounds until dawn
My thick frame was soaking with sweat
But you say you don't mind
Sending me into ecstasy away from life's unkind
It was so hot, about 120 degrees between us, no lie
This was about 5 years ago, sometime in July...

~PHOENIX

FROM DUSK TILL MOAN

EXTREME CONTENT

Your body is so intense
More euphoric than these incense
Tonight, I lost my fingers inside myself
A quarter after the hour of the twelfth
My mouth is wet with the fantasy combination of
rum & cum
and I'd like to…
Come and be ravished by you…
Your hands on me…
Dick got me grindin' against a memory
Release me from this rusted cage another called 'Love'
I will forewarn you; I like it a lil rough
I am the gateway of subliminal erotica
I ain't nobody's carbon copy or replica
You knew exactly from the start
That you were fuckin' with the Queen
I reign seduction, and it's exactly what it seems
Every word that hangs from my well-glossed lips
Not just the ones above the neck, but below the hips
Guilty! Ms. Phoenix loves her some action.
Don't be alarmed, it's a modest attraction
Reciprocate my melody, I want your verbal penetration
Bust a rhyme on my tongue
For an intimate demonstration
Short of breath and my knees instantly weak
Wanting you so deep, I can't even speak

FROM DUSK TILL MOAN

As you can see, I am literary erotic
I'm a simple freak, need nothing exotic
I just need you to assemble your body inside of mine
Then maybe we can do a little 6, 9...
I'm not asking you to put marital promises in the air
I'm asking you to pull my fucking hair
I'm not asking you for flowers and affection
I'm asking you to give me some direction
Do I crawl on my knees, or do I bend over this bed?
Do I raise one leg or squat instead?
I'm not a one hitter quitter and that's all she wrote
I am the Captain, I'm riding the fucking boat
I'll swallow all of the fantasies you have ever had
All the things they refused, I'd be glad
Demand it!
Assert & consent
And don't apologize for the Extreme Content

~PHOENIX

FROM DUSK TILL MOAN

GRAND RISING

Wake up Love.
Quietly attractive and radiating intelligence
Shy but made up of erotic sense
Rise Love.
Summon me to follow your days' journey
Release and let your magic adorn me
Mercury is ruling so I want to consider thee
Your ascendants are sensitive to any discomforting
Earth Love.
Seducing from the soles of your feet.
Stirring up an awakening no man can compete
Your energy is purposeful and trustworthy
You have my permission no need for an attorney
Moon Love.
Thank you for your protection
Positively flowing and you are my awakening
Making love is far from forsaking
I welcome you and pray to your spirit
Moaning in enchantment, I hope that you hear it
Wake Up Love.

~PHOENIX

SEDUCTION

Looking at my face and body trembling
hoping to arouse you more
Sitting at full attention and throbbing
outside of your pants, I'm sure
Undo your zipper and make love to me
at the red light
The streets are empty,
not a soul in sight
Our lips meet and spark
that oak wood that you own
Setting our bodies ablaze
and every part shown
Our lips seduce each other like old lovers
The southern comfort of a man,
no need for covers
Immediately dividing my legs to moisten me
with the tip of your middle finger
My hood valiantly protects the clit
like the Masked Singer
Moaning pleasurably as my wetness
affirms your actions
Willing to risk it all for public indecency,
minor infractions
Reaching all eight thousand nerve endings apparently
Got me speaking gibberish incoherently
Feeling seduced in the only way one should do
I mean I just wanna, I just wanna, I just wanna
Ooo....
Profanity that escaped my full lips
making you want to slide inside of them

FROM DUSK TILL MOAN

Exhilarating, undeniable chemistry
that we've refused to condemn
The first thrust was the best
as we gasped at the same time
Like taking a shot of Patron without salt or lime
Not sure how much time has lapsed
while we savor each muscle
Interrupting your world,
you should've known I was trouble....

~PHOENIX

FROM DUSK TILL MOAN

FROM DUSK TILL MOAN

The magic in a flesh memory, is that though my mind may forget you, my body never will. This is both a gift... And a curse.

~Anu

FROM DUSK TILL MOAN

FROM DUSK TILL MOAN

EVERY MORNING

5 A.M... Your body shifting out of REM was something I've been anticipating for about 15 minutes now... While you tell me I can wake you in this manner... Your resting features are the most beautiful... And the most truthful... It being a joy to watch to you... Self-fulfilling prophecies I uttered right before we slipped into bed... Right after watching a rerun of CHICAGO MED... Is it weird that crime and medical dramas do something to me?

We sink into each other more than we do the couch... Our emotions open to motion capture, raptured and transported to being a live studio audience... This is what we are into. Our mental connection projects a wide panorama. We are hot chocolate & flannel pajamas... Cheesy...

I didn't even want to ruin the perfect post work evening. Your head hit my chest harder than any pillow and you stayed there, my figure held prisoner for 5 hours...

5 A.M Once more... You turn over. I feel you stir in your subconscious, reaction to the stimulus of my eyes opening... Groping me for about 10 seconds, teasing my release by turning over and returning back to sleep...

My manhood wags in a tantrum... "Down boy," ... He's back hard. A pit bull watching his owner leave the house from the back yard... I would much rather gag your throat than do the shake weight motion... A unanimous vote that the moment you woke... It's going to be the last person getting dressed... The slowest poke you ever felt in your life... I made you my wife this way it will forever linger... I slide into you like a ring on a wedding finger.

PAGE 23

FROM DUSK TILL MOAN

The last thing the moon heard was the 1st thing the sun seen... The morning walking in on my thumb in your ass... Orgasm leaving our thighs shining in the sun... Illuminating this otherwise dark room, distorting the negatives... I dig you until your legs are stiff, then after I massage them, I spread em to preserve the jelly I'm always ready for... We walk confidently into the day we are headed for... Knowing 5 A.M comes every morning.

~ANU

FROM DUSK TILL MOAN

FUCK YOU/FUCK YOU

I haven't spoken to you in weeks...
you haven't spoken to me either,
neither has there been any attempt on our parts.
In the back of my mind,
I know what I know and I feel how I feel.
And I said what I said.
Every day I face the cold reality of this lonely space
in a bed constructed by pure, unadulterated... longing.
I resent you. I don't hate you, don't mistake this stalemate
to involve anything but resolve...
but this wall has 2 weak points...
and I don't know if it's strong enough to...
hold back the undeniable fact...
that it's fuck you... and I wanna fuck you.

It's tough to digest...
in the midst of this wild west scenario...
a scary show of unnecessary force is turning me...
the fuck on.
My solitude filled with the phantom cries
of my name coming from your lips.
Echoes of our bodies quaking require no faking...
My face breaking its stoicism to remember how
dismembered our bodies parts were...
Scattered all over the bed like imperfect star fish,
a hard wish from this hard shit,
cocked in nostalgia,

FROM DUSK TILL MOAN

ready to gouge your fountain in pure perverted passion.
The fashion is utterly informal,
nothing normal can come from this,
nothing ever has,
the past has told me & me and & me again
what I'm so willing to ignore for all of 60 minutes...
and no more.
Any more than that and once again
I gave you more than you'll give me and
reliving the panic of impending insanity had me
questioning the man in me... and because of this...
it's FUCK YOU!
but in this very moment...
right here...
I wanna FUCK you.
My adrenaline wants to rush you...
no time for you to pass or bail...
this is no longer pass or fail...
but a not waiting if the shoe fits kinda blitz.
Every exit covered, the rock and the hard place
I'm about to subject you to... unprotected too...
raw skin to skin... in and deeper in...
First sink then swim
into that place only I am familiar with.
Feel me fill you,
fear I'd kill you if I didn't still love the fuck out of you...
choking you tight enough but loose enough to control
your breathing with every thrust.
Trust imma show you what you lost,
how this moment is worth way more than it cost,

FROM DUSK TILL MOAN

the back shots alone got a Vicky-overtone.
Our moans halted by you faltering to your stomach...
nah, run it...bring that ass back up like a cheating scandal.
Handle it the way you should have
and maybe we would have gotten through this stupid shit... but we didn't.
I gave everything, while you only gave enough to...
have me at this point where it's all middle fingers...
FUCK YOU!
but in this very moment I wanna take these fingers,
put them in your pussy, and slowly finger fuck you.

~ANU

THIRSTY

I wanna sip your pussy like it's coming from a glass,
Make your river run and form a pool under your ass,
Make you cream and squirt while leaving handprints on your thighs...
Those aren't tears you're crying
You're just cumming out your eyes.

~ANU

FROM DUSK TILL MOAN

#MOOD

Don't ask me what I'm doing.
Don't ask me why I'm growling.
Moving slowly but assertive.
Looking like I'm prowling when I remove your shirt
Then give your nipples a gentle pinch
Bite your cheek then lick your face
Just to make your pussy clench...
I'm in that type of mood.
You aren't about to tell me no.
You reach down and palm it...
Feel it stiffen...
Watch it grow...
It's done being complacent
It's about to make a statement
In all body languages.
This a channel you ain't changing
But you're squeezing the remote
Your walls need painting
And your throat is naked
They both need a coat .
You give me north face while facing south
Dick encased in your amazing mouth
You slobber as I take it out,

FROM DUSK TILL MOAN

Me and your pussy lips start making out.

You're otw

So am I

You open wide

I go inside

I meet your soul

It cums outside.

~ANU

FROM DUSK TILL MOAN

PSA (PARANORMAL SEXUAL ACTIVITY)

I should have handled this differently. I know better now to never let you go to bed angry again. To never let you sit with this frown that I've always found to be just as beautiful as your smile... But I know better now. As I lay here looking at the ceiling fan do its revolution on its axis...I and my body responding to this phantom groping. I can feel your hands tugging at my waistband, undoing the drawstring, freeing my shackled manhood as it rises from its cloth cage and stands at full attention in the light. I'm not even surprised by our paranormal sexual activity. And neither are you. I'm in your face. My nose is touching yours, our lips are close enough to touch but far enough to distinguish whose face is whose. I choke you up against the wall. You're still angry, and so am I. You swing at me. I dodge the wide arc of it and press your body between mine and the wall. Fuck talking, fuck arguing, just... Fuck. Engulfing your face, you try to push me away, but my tongue has something to say that you need to feel, from the roof of your mouth to the tip of your chin, from the tip of your chin down to your breast, that now tremble with nipples as erect as I am... You are stuck now. Paralyzed by a mixture of intimidation and exhilaration. Your breaths are increasingly loud. I'm ripping at your clothes, emancipating all of your curves, as I take down the leggings you are wearing, my mouth finds my favorite place in the whole wide world, and I bury my face in you while you stand. Your juices are coming down as I eat you standing up. My hand still clutched to your throat as my tongue does its excavation, scooping you out of you and

FROM DUSK TILL MOAN

into me. Your body goes limp as you squirt down my throat and down my chin, cream forming an Oreo and milk like mustache on my profile.

~ANU

LUNCHBREAK

All work and no play has been the rule of the weeks passing... the lasting of this drought got a real nigga going haywire. Work. Home. Sleep. Repeat. I haven't seen you in a while. I'm in your vicinity on assignment. Perfect alignment of timing so I send you a text, hoping you're available around a little after noon. I let you know I'm at work but I'm about to go on break soon. I tell you I have an hour and it's too late for brunch. You reply that you got me and you're bringing me lunch. You ask me what do I want. I say I want something warm and wet. I can hear you smile through the phone before you hang up. Now I'm watching time. Every second that goes by, extending the way I am right now, just thinking about what you may have in mind. The sun is shining high through the window... as I walk outside to the parking lot, you pull up to the curb in an all-black truck. You tip your shades a little and smirk. I can't help but grin ear to ear like a Cheshire cat... my eyes disappearing in my smile... you look at me then look at the parking deck. I jump into the backseat, and you pull off with an umph! I peer over the driver seat to see what you're wearing... realizing your shirt doesn't have a bottom... but what turns me on the most is your freshly painted lavender colored toenails. My manhood growls louder than my stomach. You pull into the parking deck and proceed to the lowest level. Cars have vacated their spaces in the lunch rush... leaving plenty of opportunity. I can't help but reach around and grope you, pulling your hair away from your neck... all respect your beautiful image being left intact goes out of car windows as we park. You get out of the car, not even bothering to pull your shirt down, your

FROM DUSK TILL MOAN

bare curvaceous figure walking to the back the trust. I follow you out of the car and around to where you are now waiting... in the trunk on all 4's, ass erect, pussy glistening, looking better than any food ad I've ever seen... I kiss your ass cheeks lovingly for supporting such a beautiful sight for sore eyes... my tongue venturing to the liquid luck in the middle... you whisper "fuck" in a giggle giving that ass a wiggle as I bury my nose in you... I suck on your clit as gently as a hungry pup sucks on a teat in anticipation of a life giving substance... I take my longest finger and let it sit at the entrance, massaging gently before I go all the way in... pull it out gently to lick the cream from my finger... the chill down your spine lets me know I'm close... your breaths become more and more rushed as I increase my pace, I don't have long even though I'm far from done... your release into my beard... moisturizing and even texturizing the normally strait hairs starting to curl... this is what I've been craving... why I been behaving so strangely... all this slaving with no savior to keep her flavor on my tongue. Lunch has been served.... and now it's back to work... she drops me off begrudgingly back in front of the office... as I get out she grabs my arm... "if you staying I got dinner for you too" before pulling off savagely from the curb.

~ANU

FROM DUSK TILL MOAN

STAR GAZERS

I been waiting all summer for a clear night sky. It came on a Sunday night... the heat in the air only lessened a little as the sun took it talents to foreign hemispheres... as the last light left the sky the moon decided to show half her ass... up close and personal... her lunar light enriching the night giving sight to an array of stars coming from their respective light years... watching... perfect. I've waited for this night and apparently so did you. My galaxy lights up and sounds off with a ding! It's you, hoping that I'm free tonight ... me not wanting to seem too ripe I make you a deal... if the stars align right within our lines of sight...then it's me you shall see . The stars like you and I... and wanting to see the show I've promised to put on for them... they take a seat front and center sky... peering down with eager twinkles. Not only did they clear their schedules... they made sure not a cloud would appear, that one person who messes up the bootleg by walking across the screen... the scene will be set.. needs will be met. Every cosmic entity is in attendance tonight, voyeurs in their own right, waiting patiently for the festivities to begin. Your skin glows faintly in the light, from a shade of macadamia to the fairest of them all, you hair, if in the sun, would look like a signal flare... a shining red now crimson in the nights touch. The 1st image I see as I pull up, the tulips planted in the front yard sway in the slight breeze, your 2 lips go from a smirk to a light cheese. Your clothes looking painted on, my eyes almost fainted climbing the spread of your thighs to encompass your hips. With an embrace of the body and a brush of the lips you had me as open as

FROM DUSK TILL MOAN

the sky tried to be, clouds attempt to crowd the stage, only to fade a few seconds later. If only they could be paid. The show is about to begin. What we are here for this very weekend requires attention... and searching. Laying on our backs on this trampoline, perching we engage into a staring match with the cosmos. We banter and snicker back and forth about who will get lucky 1st to see a streak. The 1st one fell between us. We saw it together. The perfect weather permitting us to make ambitious wishes. The moon pulled up her pants a little, hinting, teasing, freezing the moment it set our bodies on fire. Our eyes went from the skies to each other. Our bodies vibrating closer to each other, the material flexing beneath us, supporting our weight as we converge to our center, a the very center of this ring we find each other, clothes peeling off, revealing the softness of your yin, to the rigidity of my yang...what covers my face next is a cloud I can grab, I stick my tongue in it, stroking the underside of your clit as I secure your thighs I trace a familiar yet foreign place my exploring of you discovers there are stars inside this space, a sexual representation of the universe inside this earthen vase. Your head snaps back and you gasp as a few more stars fall out of orbit. Absorbing the friction that you lend me, my mouth enters into a frenzy, trying to get the same stars to fall out of you. As the clouds form again the light falls out of view, but for what its worth we're on another star search. Our current position of the cancer commission. Spit sliding down my pole like its performing, you do to my dick what I do to your clit. Your throat giving my inside a wormhole treatment, making my body capable of interstellar travel. Before we unravel we twist tighter, a challenging battle between a lover and a fighter, I squeeze into you with a

FROM DUSK TILL MOAN

submission move. Our mouths devouring, ravenous, our abdomens slapping against. The trampoline under us adds a bounce to every ounce. Every thrust gaining locomotive force. I wrap your hair inside my fist and give it a jerk, causing you and me to both go berserk. I take it out of you and slap it against your jaw. You purred an "ooh" and looked up and what had me shook up is how the moon started to strip, and just lit up. You wanna moon the moon the now. I stuck between 2 round light asses, the stars pulled out their phones and now they're turning up in masses. You bring it back like a December 31st, 1999, we just may get caught, have to pay a mighty fine, because I got you screaming out your breathing, there's every bit of reason to be this loud, and for the rest of the night we didn't see another cloud. We both came a second time, forgetting to count the falling stars, so we simply settled to watch the moon get fucked by Mars.

~ANU

FROM DUSK TILL MOAN

Like water, be formless and free. Be deeper than the abyss.

~Danovel

FROM DUSK TILL MOAN

FROM DUSK TILL MOAN

VIEW YOU

Please Goddess allow me to view you
What I mean by view you
Play with your love like a guitar,
I don't care where we are
couch, balcony, or car

I view you as the Star

Discretion is thoroughly advised,
thus a mental movie is quite warranted

Those little strokes you love to make with your
middle finger to your clitoris
Always making me quite wet, I love how you do it

I'm going to record you, it will not be forgotten
How swollen she was or how tender she becomes

As you caress her at a steady speed,
freely spilling out your woman seed
I intend to bow to my knees to show gratitude

Ferociously sucking and licking
at the seemingly flowing nectar
I may be wrong for reaping the harvest,
as I didn't do the work

You're as juicy as a blackberry tree,
sweeter than strawberry jelly
I cannot take pride in this masterpiece,
full of jealousy

FROM DUSK TILL MOAN

You would grip the back of my head
and let me know it was so good
I'm going to always be your only fan
If you allow me to view you

~DANOVEL

FROM DUSK TILL MOAN

LITTLE VICKY SECRET

Affectionately called my Little Vicky Secret
Always surprised by the freaky lingerie she would wear
She said it was her pleasure to put them on whenever
I was in the atmosphere
Undressing her with my eyes, yes sex is in the air

I took pride in removing one bra strap
to devour her ripened nipple
Then I broke out a feather for a pleasurable tickle
Licking and sucking upon her ass, allowing easy access
Little Vicky Secret had no fight in her
She was willing to be my little freak night or day
Willing to be my sexual slave,
tying her up to the bedpost

Bending her legs back,
pounding her relentlessly as she became a fountain
Tonguing her asshole
while it was my face she was mounting and drowning

Begging to be licked, sucked, fucked and ate right
Little Vicky Secret was seeing stars and galaxies
and it wasn't even night

FROM DUSK TILL MOAN

I dove in her and went swimming
Hadn't even seen a pool this past summer
Baby girl didn't just remind me of a jeep
she the whole damn hummer

Never a snack, always an entrée
She should just come over naked, Fuck the Lingerie

~DANOVEL

FROM DUSK TILL MOAN

SEXUAL ALIGNMENT

Having the audacity to conduct a test
I invited spiritual bae over for some spiritual sex
I am the guru
and between her legs exists the highest offering
But not without the oil diffuser, crystals & sage
Performing rituals naked, physically sexing me mentally
Amazing, we danced the dance of soul mates
Always feening for soul quenching fucking
But not before blazing
Setting her mouth upon my Yoni, it was like Magic
A moth to a flame, spellbound if you will
Immediately wanting and needing to scream her name
Oh, it was a sex that soothed the soul
Feminine as she, I was aggressively swallowed whole
Riding me with a vengeance her eyes never left mines
Added my right hand to her neck
and my left gripping her thigh
Nothing but thrusting, moans, groans, and peering
Her eyes finally roll to the back of her head
Vaginal muscles gripping and pulsating strong and deep
Our sacral chakras now aligned
Shall we repeat

~DANOVEL

LUST AT DAWN

Dawn has awakened us at an ungodly hour tracing my finger along her hourglass shape. Spontaneous, lustful thoughts swirling around my head My clitoris already throbbing, desiring her I pull her body unto mine. Now we become intertwined even though it is no longer bedtime. As I caress her body, soft moans leave her lips. She sways her hips as the sensation overcomes her. Bringing me in for soft and sensual kisses. I rub the sleep out of her eyes, then proceed to spread her legs to scoop out whatever dew was left from last night's rendezvous. Licking her off my fingers, I prepare to make more. As I enter, her back arches allowing easy access. Yes, I love morning sex! It's when I'm most ready. All in her like sauce in spaghetti, tossed in her as if I was dressing. And she is the salad. Steady rocking to the break of dawn, she knows she turns me on. Our bodies can never seem to part. I just discreetly, but inadvertently touch her heart with each stroke I effortlessly tame her, In the Morning

~DANOVEL

FROM DUSK TILL MOAN

FROM DUSK TILL MOAN

FROM DUSK TILL MOAN

My river flowed endlessly for the onslaught of kisses you gave. You, I craved. ~Aria Knox

FROM DUSK TILL MOAN

FROM DUSK TILL MOAN

COLLIDE

I craved the feel of you deep inside my soul
Watched your lips move with synchronicity
As I caved and gave into the hold
let my guard down as you held me

Writhed in my seat as I felt the thick air
Cut off my breath
Thoughts of entangled sheets
crept in my mind under your glare

I just wanted your hands splayed upon my back
Sipping hot coffee,
desperately trying to put my mind on track.

The cool, late fall night didn't extinguish the heat
transferred from your body to mine
I allowed my head to fall back as you traced my ear with
your tongue, sending chills down my spine.

I needed you then, now and ever.

Anxiously offering what I should not redeem,
But tonight, I'd exist in this moment
One we lost, long ago, And hold onto the dream.

Butterflies fluttered in my stomach as I waited for you.
Praying to the gods that I don't rethink this, don't think...

Containing emotions, carefully I let you in and opened
myself to you. Our lips touched and the magic of the
moment grew.

Mmm...the timbre of your voice against my clenched
teeth, positioned you closer to me.

FROM DUSK TILL MOAN

You grazed my erect nipple with your finger and a whimper of pleasure escaped my lips.

Knees weak, you held me in place.

Gently, inched me back and took a dip.

My river flowed endlessly for the onslaught of kisses you gave. You, I craved.

Possessively holding my thighs, I remembered what being yours felt like, understood the consequence of withholding from you,

I moaned into the night, as you kissed further.

I wouldn't disobey you, responded when you said to.

Never to lose control, you entered me with precision. Rode me slowly, and carefully, I had visions...of this intensity, And I basked for one night only.

Your touch reminding me what femininity feels like, whispering how you've missed me, and I you.

Never selfish, assuredly taking care.
My body quaked, you urged me to run if I dared.

I reacted to your firm thrusts
and buried my nails into your back.
You arched and moaned, keeping your pace intact.

Tightly my thighs wrapped around you as passion guided your fingers gently around my neck...I gasped and fell victim to the thrill.

Heavily breathing against your cheek, kissing your chest, you found my lips again, singing my name into my soul as

FROM DUSK TILL MOAN

if I were unfamiliar with the sound.
Chance encounters and yearning for you drowned.

We climbed to the top of mount ecstasy and
Stared at each other under the amber glow of lit candles.
Tasted the sweetness of love
made by two souls trapped in a parallel universe.
Held onto the feeling of satiation that we knew first.

I trained my heart to forgive my body for the ride.
And we'll remember the moment we chose to forego
logic and collide.

~ARIA KNOX

DANGER ZONE

You live to feel my lips pressed against your neck as you writhe beneath me and align your back, erect.
This glow upon you, incandescent
Matching the mood of the atmosphere where kaleidoscopic pictures burst before you in ecstasy...enchanted.

Might we taste the flavor of each other's fruit and be driven to a place where fantasies bloom.
As I am enthralled by you and the feel of your skin burns my soul with each seductive move.
I'm envious of the fabrics that graze your body, making a mockery of me and my inability to touch your silky smooth.... I curse the very delicates that cover you, deeming it impossible for me to be that close, but soon...

I'll delve deeper into your pulsating river, afloat a wave I'll ride with vigor....

For adoring the essence of someone never felt as intoxicating as this lesson.
You teach with careful consideration
and I listen intently in admiration.

As if this love could transcend us to a place unknown, I'll trace kisses along your spine, dangerously in the zone.

~ARIA KNOX

FROM DUSK TILL MOAN

G SPOT

We fuck with feverish urgency,

Grabbing, sucking, wildly crumpling sheets.

My abstract mind draws mental pictures of your pleasure spots on a canvas of black skin.

The elevated art of your tattoos delight my tongue...

As the feel and salty taste of your flesh makes my body quake at the onslaught of this drunken love, come.
Pinch me...my risen chocolate buds erect for you
Caught in a daze at the thought of my body
being your muse.
Could I brand you with imprints of light bites?

Graze my teeth over your smooth...

Forbidden fruits I dare to invade,
Purposefully crying out to the heavens, your name.
Your breath caught mid moan, holding tightly to the small of my back as we ride this wave.
Pointed toes on silk sheets, I open my treasure box, you find your way.

Hands through your hair as if I could touch your mind, filling the air with the scent of passion. I'm draped in sweat and haughty arrogance of this love...lasting
Beyond the seconds and minutes it took to disrobe,
I just wanna feel your deep stroke, probe...me...
Into the position you like best,
Mine is ass up, you tweaking my breasts.

FROM DUSK TILL MOAN

You love to see me, in all my glory
Deeper baby, deeper, my river flows as you're exploring.
Lipstick smudged, scratches and tousled hair
I writhe beneath you,
desperately praying you keep it right there...

Make a move, show me what you got,
I'm opened wide, oh shit, that's my spot.
Evidence is written on the walls
where my red polish stains.
Starving for your touch
only you can ease my hunger pains.

Come towards me and cum for me,
In your eyes I stare as we meld together.
Won't you disrobe me?
I need you like I need air in my lungs
Taste me baby, my velvet smooth on your tongue.

I'll coax you with the warmth of my thighs,
Build a bridge to ecstasy as my back arches in time
In sync, we move and groove
to the sounds of our own music.
Let me run my fingers through your hair
and grab ahold of the love waiting there.

When you capture the sweetness of my chocolate kiss,
Your soul I peruse and can't resist.
I'm in love with the way you do you...
I'll be your tabletop confection,
Stretch my body and soon
I'll unfold in your arms

~ARIA KNOX

FROM DUSK TILL MOAN

UNTITLED

Proceed with caution
The words I play in my mind
But I want those lips tenderly on mine
I could play coy and pretend I want the real
But my body betrays me and begs for the thrill
Our tongues meet and I want yours deeper
Invade my cavern, surely you'll be a keeper
The rise of my breath as you trail through my valley below
Fall on your chest as our rhythm moves slow
I inhale you and memorize your feel beneath my hands
Finding my home safe and sound in this erotic love land
Tip your head back so I may lick you to my heart's content
Drawing pictures on your collarbone
Come until you're spent.
Ease the lacy playthings gently from my hips
Allow your feathery kisses to meet my supple lips.
Sending shockwaves through me
as you effortlessly part my thighs
I'm lost in the abyss of ecstasy deep within your eyes.
Stir me baby, don't go too slow

FROM DUSK TILL MOAN

Keep this rhythm and hear me moan

Mm, I scream your name for the world to hear

Love me baby harder and whisper in my ear.

You love my rolling hills and unselfishly I give it

Taste my sweetness, there's so much you've been missing

Don't you like my flavor, covering you so?

Allow to me to arch my back and let the river flow.

Hone in on my language, read me loud and clear

I want you now not later, enter me right here.

We'll get high on the moment

Take me baby, get your fill

Climax in unison...ooh I want you Still.

Now we can go around on the carousel you see

But I would much rather you open my lock with your key.

Set me ablaze as only you can

Imagine my cries of passion over and over and over again

~ARIA KNOX

FROM DUSK TILL MOAN

FROM DUSK TILL MOAN

FROM DUSK TILL MOAN

To every lover who did not incite me to poetry........

Shame on you. ~KatandraShanel

FROM DUSK TILL MOAN

FROM DUSK TILL MOAN

GOOD TILL THE LAST…

Sticky

Sweet

Saccharine

Juices flowing out of me and into your open mouth.
Your face pressed hard against my pussy.
And you're careful not to waste a single drop.

~K. SHANEL

PUSSY PICS

Tell me you love it and you can't wait to talk to it
Your mouth to those lips. Tell me you can't wait
To tease it.... touch it.... taste it.... tear into it....
treat it like the best you ever had.... pretend it's the first....
pray it's the last............
Tell me you can't wait to meet her.

~K. SHANEL

FROM DUSK TILL MOAN

LOVE SLAVE

My pussy in the palms of your hands
She is I and I am she
Me and my pussy

Throbbing
Dripping

Held captive in the palms of your hands
You spread the lips and squeeze the clit

You spank her
Slow then fast
Soft then hard

You insert your ring and middle fingers
And in a come hither motion
You tease my G-spot
You laugh as my pussy tightens
You abruptly withdraw your fingers
You tell me you're not here to please me
It is I who was born to please you
Hands and knees is the position to assume

Head back
Mouth open
Eye to eye

As you push your dick inside
Past my teeth and over my tongue
This is what you came for
You rub your dick across my lips
Your eyes demanding me to taste you as I lick the tip

FROM DUSK TILL MOAN

Your hands grip my hips as you turn me around
A knowing nudge against my cheeks
And it's ass up face down
I squirm as I anticipate the moment you penetrate
As you push into me I cry out in vain
Your hands have me securely by the waist
In and out. In and out. You thrust.
Your dick swollen. Your seed spilling as you bust.
I'm delirious with the onslaught of pleasure and pain.

Body bound
Mind enslaved

I was born to please you....

~K. SHANEL

CLIMAX (GRADATIO)

I want to moan your name while the weight of you presses into me. While the weight of you presses into me the contour of my body leaves an imprint on Egyptian cotton sheets. On Egyptian cotton sheets you fuck me. You fuck me like you're Akhenaten and I am Nefertiti. I am Nefertiti the Nile flowing from my pussy. My pussy dripping and gripping and devouring every inch of you. Every inch of you disappearing into me claiming me. Claiming me as the weight of you presses into me......

~K. SHANEL

FROM DUSK TILL MOAN

FROM DUSK TILL MOAN

PAGE 69...

FROM DUSK TILL MOAN

FROM DUSK TILL MOAN

Out of nowhere here you come. Teasing me. I just found myself waking up around 3 a.m with a hard on wanting to enter into you. ~Vino Davis

FROM DUSK TILL MOAN

FROM DUSK TILL MOAN

HEY YOU... It's crazy how you're always on my mind at crazy hours... It's really soooo much more to it... But it's always sooooo raw and uncut... And beautiful. When I try to make sense of it, and, or try to put it into words... I always ruin it or it never comes close to describing the beauty of if... If that makes sense.

2:17 A.M :: In and out of sleep... Visions of laying behind you in a spooning position... Reach both hands in front of you and softly cup both your breasts... Play with your nipples until you are aroused... Breathing softly, warmly on the back of your neck... As I whisper in your ear, "I want you soooo bad"... But you already know, because you can feel the stiffness of my manhood pressing against your ass...

2:24 A.M :: The thought of being inside you, well, the thought of fucking you... Running through my head now... A gazillion women in the world and presently I'm focused on YOU... WHY? The thought of... STOP!!! SLOW DOWN... I'm too excited, extra sensitive and I'm about to cum inside of you... NO!!!!... I'm NOT READY... I want to stroke you slow... all the way in and all the way out... sooooo you can feel ALL OF ME... As you call out my name... "You feel so fuck'n good inside me"... Just listening to you speak those words.... Almost made me lose my load inside you... As I roll off you... Because if I had not... I would have came... The thought of the tightness of you working and squeezing your pussy muscles around me was too much to bear... As I lay on my back... You straddle me and direct my penis into your dripping wet hot pussy... You're in full control now... As I palm both sides of your ass cheeks... Reaching up to put your breasts into my mouth... You moan... You call my name again... "I'm about tooo.... Tooo.... I'm cumming..." I feel your juices running down my thighs... I softly roll you over... Spread your legs... And put my mouth on your clitoris... Your back arches as you moan in pure pleasure... "I'm cumming again" you stutter those words...

2:31 A.M :: .Soooo you went back to sleep after leaving me with a hard ass dick..... When all I could think about was feeling your tightness around me as you wrap your legs around my back controlling my in and out motion... Every time you pull me close, deep inside your sweet loving garden... Moaning my name with each stroke, it's taking every mental muscle in my build NOT to explode deep inside you... After months and months of dreaming of this pussy.... I can hold back NO LONGER.... I pull back and pull out... You grab my penis with your hand and insert it in your warm mouth.... Instantly I nut everywhere... Your face, your neck, your breast.......... You smile proudly knowing how much control you displayed over my cumming.... G'night ....

3:33 A.M :: Why you all up in my head?....It's crazy how I be thinking about.... Wanting to roll over and pull you close to me and slide inside you....

~VINO DAVIS

FROM DUSK TILL MOAN

FROM DUSK TILL MOAN

OUTRO

Your tongue coaxing me into submission as my pussy throbs for you, aches for you. Your mouth is amazing, except, I crave depth. You are more than happy to oblige.

Nail prints on your back, I open wide for your fill. Pussy pulsating for the engorged, you, stroke me to the hilt.

Stretching... Erotic possessing... Evoke until I tilt. From my ceiling to my basement. Orgasms are built.

Moans of ecstasy plaster the walls like paint. The neighbors know you by the crescendo of your name. As I ride each glorious orgasm like a wave. Crashing into the abyss, our melodious song in the atmosphere. Spreading my limbs to another hemisphere.

~A COMPOSITION BY ANU, ARIA KNOX & K.SHANEL

FROM DUSK TILL MOAN

TO BE CONTINUED...

Hot & heavy sex with you

Petting, panting, pressure

With our clothes on like them young'uns do

The old folks called it "hunching"

But we grown now

Zippers down

Finger fucking

Two finger thrusting

Back & forthing

Your fingers making my pussy drip

My fingers wrapped around your dick

From the base to the tip

Jeans being pushed past my hips

Thighs, ankles, floor

As I beg for more....

~K.SHANEL

FROM DUSK TILL MOAN

FROM DUSK TILL MOAN

ALSO BY FREEDOMINK PUBLISHING

Woman on Fire by Trinette Collier

Love Continuum by Ja'Maela Byrd writing as Aria Knox

Teach Me by Phoenix

Can't Raise No Man by Katandra Jackson Nunnally*

COMING SOON TO FREEDOMINK PUBLISHING

Nakíd by Ja'Maela Byrd writing as Aria Knox

Magnolia by Phoenix

Sunsets On Mars by Katandra Shanel*

FROM DUSK TILL MOAN

Printed in the USA
CPSIA information can be obtained
at www.ICGtesting.com
LVHW030736050424
776403LV00007B/484

9 780989 678698